THE IMMIGRANT'S CONTRACT

THE IMMIGRANT'S CONTRACT

poems by
Leland Kinsey

DAVID R. GODINE
Publisher · Boston

DAVID R. GODINE, *Publisher*
Post Office Box 450
Jaffrey, New Hampshire 03452
www.godine.com

LIBRARY OF CONGRESS
CATALOGING-IN-PUBLICATION DATA

Kinsey, Leland.
The immigrant's contract : poems / by Leland Kinsey.
p. cm.
ISBN-13: 978-1-56792-353-7
ISBN-10: 1-56792-353-4
1. Immigrants—Poetry. 2. Acculturation—Poetry. I. Title.
PS3561.I5737I46 2008
811´.54—DC22
2007046814

FIRST EDITION
Printed in the United States

CONTENTS

THE IMMIGRANT'S CONTRACT

The Still Houses

we rode past,
and those we then rode past more than once,
on the way to those that still showed signs
of the living – smoke in the chimney,
movement by a door or shed or barn,
held dead unattended and the doctor knew
what their god's hand had laid low
would not be mustered up by his
and only the sextons' hands
would lay them lower.
I would pull the horses up
where lives waxed or waned;
the doctor would step out,
often after waking,
to anger, gushing, despair,
and try to repair the rents in the fabric of the world,
any larger handiwork hidden in the ill-knit weave
and he on the fell-line like my mother at her loom,
the day's work. One morning
the doctor certified two brothers
who had married sisters, and the women walked
from opposite sides of town
and met in the middle and immediately knew
a certainty.
The doctor often one to play
on other days. Other seasons,
he would have me stop where the street widened
as the river gulf did to fit the town
laid astride the gorge to capture its power.
In the wide street he would join the boys –
most of whom he'd brought into the world,
many of whom he was now seeing off –
playing ball – feed-sack bases,

1

locally lathed bats made in a shop
father had worked at for a time
though he'd never played or heard of the game
before this town – almost the whole team
with one name, even the armless mascot
who cheered his brothers and cousins on
against town team rivals or factory hands.
Carloads would stop to watch.
Farmers in wagons would slow for a look,
grocers and shopkeepers near their windows
on days when playing wasn't work but hard
under a searing hard blue sky,
the kind of blue the dead now turned.
Horsehide, ash, time itself it seemed, now put by.
What nostrums and kindness the doctor had
became watered-down over time
a weak brew served in rooms with cracked-plaster
        ceilings,
or high-oak coffered ones, and young dead.
Doctor worked seven days and nights a week
so I didn't go to church, though I saw
the priest more often than when I went.
I'd enjoyed his stories, but now his voice
was like metal on a whetstone,
chipped and sharp; his face like my father's
dough; his alb like cheesecloth.
My youngest uncle came back from the war,
back from the front and the back, he said,
and from hospitals for the gas.
His breathing reminded me of the dying
around here, the sound of a boot
sinking quickly in mud.
He said he couldn't tell

the difference on the wards,
where he'd spent weeks,
between those dying from gas attacks
and those dying of flu.
He wouldn't talk of the other soldiers,
but said the landscape died
like the ash covered hills we once saw
along the Jacques-Cartier
where a forest fire had rivered out
after burning thousands of hectares
and any homes on that bank.
He said the smell was worse in France,
like you stuck your head up a cow's ass
and the cow died.
He couldn't work in the mill
that supported the town
because the lacquer and sawdust
would have varnished his lungs up good,
mill floor and forest floor
would be too much, and farmer's lung
would've killed him if he worked in barns.
He ended up tending roads for the town,
riding the horse-drawn hone in summer,
the winged plow in winter,
or walking behind to keep warm.
I drove those roads, frozen to dust
or thawed to ruts, all that fall
so the doctor could rest
behind the buggy's weather sheet.
The doctor's horses had soft mouths
so the lines running between my fingers
required little pressure, only direction.
I watched the fiery landscape darken,

3

smelled the leaves turning to mold,
felt the clench in my gut like a punch.
Once a fall thunderstorm exploded trees
from a ridge by the road;
the horses bolted; I sawed the lines
to bring them in, but they picked up their heads
took the bits and drove ahead faster
till his hand came from behind the rubberized cotton
and seemed to no more than touch the lines
and the horses calmed; the hand withdrew.
We were riding through the town I'd known
most of my life since my family'd arrived
in a horse-drawn wagon,
including my older sister, now numbered among
        the dead.
The town constable had stopped us
and said it was cruel and unusual punishment
for the horse to pull such a load
of family and furniture,
this after trucks and cars were known
but not where we came from,
north of the Eastern Townships,
and that long trip had been hard
on all of us, horse included,
and the constable threw my father in jail
for the night, but the justice let him go
in the morning, said he was already where
the horse would do a horse's work.
And my father left it at that,
but told me years later he wanted
to put a spade in the constable's temple,
but said frogs don't kill the hawk.

FROGS

we were, for years.
I learned English at school and on the streets
and taught my parents in the evening,
read them newspapers, textbooks, and magazines
from the Carnegie library on Second Street,
paid for by a man my father said should be blessed
and shot. If radio had existed
they would have learned easier.
We survived for a time.
Farming French parents often never learned,
kids stuck in the past at home,
held to a narrower future at school,
but my father wanted to open a bakery shop.
He worked odd jobs around town,
creamery, cheese factory, feed store.
Everywhere *Frog* or *Frenchie*
till they finally used his name
as they came to know him.
My mother tended the kitchen garden
of *haricots verts*, cornichon cucumbers,
shallots, dandelions, *mâche* or cornsalad.
The climate, though tough, was better
here, but she still quoted *her* mother,
"Go hungry in a dry year,
starve in a wet one."
She made some spring and summer meals
from the bullfrogs I jigged
with red flannel on a string
in the swamps and ponds and beaver bogs
I also fished for our trout meals.
I'd chop the hind legs off the frogs
on the same maple block I used for chickens.

I plunged old broom handles
into those same soft-bottomed ponds
and mucky shores till I hit something hard
and dredged up snapping turtles
for *ma mère* to make terrapin soup,
though often what I hit were pieces
of old rafts, slimy boards and short beams
slapped together for fishing,
or hardwood logs of long ago timber cuts
drowned from booms cabled down dammed ponds
or sunk from frozen landings
that broke early before the drive.
The turtles I found came out
of the mire and water with deep
hisses in the back of their throats
and those sharp beaks ready to snap
anything hard, or off. I carried them home
in an old pannier they chewed
up over the years, ash splints
and willow withes nothing to them.

My father finally garnished enough
from our thin living to build his business.
He laid up his stone oven – ordinary bricks above
firebox bricks below, all plastered over
as carefully as a child's room.
It stood as a small addition
to the shop's exterior wall –
and earned the family's keep
off *memé's* recipes,
the names of breads and patisseries
reminding customers of our origins.

I played ball as awkwardly as a land toad;
croaked my pleas to girls in a breaking voice;
went to school with ashes on my forehead,
and wore a toque for warmth. The toque
also from *memé's* hand
which never laid on me again
as it worked lifelong on the Saint-Laurent River's
North Shore, even greyer latitudes than here.
My grandparents' house was within bombardment
distance of the water as Wolfe had proved
with his cannonades of many villages
north of Quebec City.
His shot soared over fields running
down to the tidal shore, and pocked
the stone farm buildings. A red roof
stands out in my mind, and in the small kitchen hall
lay the long beggar's box
like a kind of battered bench.
The top and side flopped open
for a sort of trundle bed
when it was their turn to care
for one of the village poor.
A shallow dark-stained trough
skirting round the opened edge
was filled with molasses
to keep the unwelcome from the house
while the vermin-infested slept.
The priest would say they gave good comfort,
but it never comforted me,
the strong smells and scanter meals
when outsiders were there,
though my family came

to almost such a state.
Winter Saturday nights, after he'd fired the ovens
for the last time before Monday morning,
the counter was lined with bean pots –
dropped off as the next day's breads
and pastries were bought –
which he put in to slowly cook
in the long cooling till families in cars and sleighs
stopped after church for their Sunday meal,
men sitting stiff in their rigs;
women, dressed the most colorful
they'd be in a week, coming in
and leaving quickly,
in the general coming and going –
the cold crunch of tires in the yard;
the hushing of runners; horse bells
like coins ringing together in the air,
but none exchanged for the service.
The pots were placed on floorboards
under robes to keep warm, and warm feet.

ALBERTA WHEAT FIELDS

needed workers, or so the flyers
coming east said. Out of school
at sixteen, I needed work.
My father put me on the train
north to Montréal. I rode into and out of
that city, stood in Prince Albert Station,
and never dared go beyond
the thin glass shield that the city hurried beyond.
The CP passed through town every day,
but on its trans-continental run
the name Canadian-Pacific made the journey
seem huge as an ocean crossing,
and I walked the train from my cheap seat
as I might've the steerage deck of a ship.
The first day was Ottawa and trees.
I grew weary of trees with no hills above.
Suddenly the landscape was torn-up earth,
stripped hummocks of black
or blackened rock, mud and pools,
like giants had fought trench warfare,
like pictures my uncle showed me,
but magnified, with great swatches
of no man's land. And just as suddenly
the sight was dimmed by the smell
that struck like a maul, as if those giants
had kicked the corpses of all the war's dead
out of their graves.
Then, past Sudbury, into the wide woods again.
We slept and woke and slept and woke
to the brush of branches
against the coach and windows;
the rush across so many rivers

9

that when we passed Lac des Milles Lacs,
I thought land of a thousand of rivers too.
Sometimes, trackside, I glimpsed tiger lilies
like my mother used to grow in the side yard,
or sometimes a quick open view
of cattail and fleur-de-lis swales
like forest edged fields of young corn,
but the beaver lodges and dams
I could see were moss and sedge covered.
I had spotted Superior early
and watched its near shore wildness
and its horizon that seemed farther away
than the end of my life. Over the waters
at sunset I saw high clouds casting a shadow
on the upper side of a ceiling of thin low clouds.
A time later the conductor announced, "Arctic Divide."
It seemed a long decline, then the woods ended
as quickly as opening jalousies
and the prairies spread beside us,
and ahead I suppose, but we moved
with a gentle rocking for hours
in the same landscape, like an eel
swimming through a algal sea.
Towns came and went. At Portage la Prairie
I recognized my ancestors' work and passage.
Was ever a moose in Moose Jaw?
By Swift Current I was astounded by pronghorns
in the sloughs and creek defiles,
and they defined swiftness – they easily outran
the train, and could outrun
the constant wind I came to know.
The land started to have relief,

long low rolls and, far to the south,
a pale blue band of hills seemed
to travel in the opposite direction,
a slow migration of what didn't belong.
Past Medicine Hat I disembarked at Brooks
and found a wagon waiting for several.
We had hours of slower, rougher travel yet.
The railroads had opened these sections
and all the new wheat farmers
were trying to open the prairie to seed.
Most rough plowing had been fall work,
now preparing the soil was the work
of teams of teams. I drove ten horses
drawing a harrow as wide as those ten horses spanned.
I walked behind the whole affair in the dust or rain,
the fourth in an offset array of five just like it.
We'd start at sunup and walk out till midday,
the lead team following a line or heading.
A Scot said in his homeland a plant
called rest-harrow would have bound us in an hour;
I waited for ledges and rocks but the disks
wheeled on, cutting for hour after stoneless hour.
A wagon met us at noon with feed and water
for horses and men in that order.
The afternoon's work was making back
the distance we'd gone out. That would be seeded
by the gang planters as we widened the field
next day. Hired by owners, we moved
from section to section to section
that the human eye could not tell the beginning
or end of, out to the whole horizon
was cut and recut to a fairly fine powder,

and those teams of huge horses seemed
large as the tight houses and all small
in the landscape. Except in the river bottoms,
you never saw a tree. Offered no transportation
by the company, many men bought
Indian ponies from the Bloods nearby.
Assiniboine and Blackfoot not far beyond
would still take horses if left available,
walking the earth in other words.
You paid five dollars for the summer,
with the unspoken understanding you set
the horse free in the fall. They'd keep track
and sell you the same one another season
if you asked, and they liked you.
One of the women was yours for the night
for two dollars. Sunday was a day
of whoring. My first time ever,
I paid for the young wife of an older man.
Her eyes were like the coal being dug
nearby if you could make it shine like a jewel.
Her small breasts fit in my wet hands,
and I sort of held her up after she flipped
me onto my back and slid onto me.
and it didn't take much action for it all
to be done from my side, though she kept
on a little for her own purposes.
Sometimes it mattered to the women,
often not, but I worked at learning
to keep it long, as were the days after.
Often enough talking would have been
almost as good as fucking, but we usually couldn't
and that threw me back years.

Except for plots of squash and corn
the ground was unturned on the reservation.
And it was little gnawed or pawed
by animals they'd known. Birds, fish,
I wondered what filled their larders.
Miles north of Brooks a wagon passed north;
stopped; driver said they needed experienced
hands with horses to haul dinosaur bones
out of the badlands. I didn't know from either,
but knew horses, and planting was ending.
The driver and I rode till the land dropped
away and we descended

INTO THE BADLANDS.

The high plains were in late light,
but the bottom of the river-, wind-, and rain-torn
gorges below us lay dark. If I'd descended
the steep hand carved road at night,
I wouldn't have realized the size
of the vestibule of hell I was entering.
The tops of crags and hills looked red,
as if moss-covered, but from the near slope I could see
it was all rusted rock, as though you'd taken
the peen of a hammer and busted
metallic stone to a pebble debris.
Here and there large pieces of the same rock
sat like birettas atop free-standing figures,
fat or thin, of rock like concrete.
Hoodoos. Minor gods to the Indians,
who, like me, hadn't known the world was so old.
Smudges fumed by the camp as we arrived,
the men sat with nets on their heads,

mosquito season, a soft storm of insects.
Sternberg, the old man himself, said they'd exposed
so many bones they'd have to trust
I was any good. Said he'd dug here
for several years now, the best dinosaur hunting
in the world. A fellow named Barnum Brown
had been earlier, but others just ruined their finds.
The Sternbergs had been called in to get the fossils
out of the difficult stone. "Barnum dug all over
my diggings in Wyoming," he said,
"and then brought his tents and act up here.
He shipped to the great museums of the world,
and the Canadians decided to keep some bones
home, and brought us in." First lessons.

The first morning I drove a team far
up a creek bed. I headed for three perfectly rounded
hills, the *tois tits* I thought, each topped
with a small stony cap like a nipple.
Their lower sides looked like beech bark
deeply scarred by bear claws. I soon lost
sight of them in the ridges, hummocks, ledges,
tunnels, and outwashes, switchbacks,
small canyons, terraces, and lofty outcrops.
Sternberg would later lend me a book
detailing the tortures of early travelers
trying to find their way across this tortuous land.
I found my way up to a ledge where a skull
lay half dug out. Teeth like bowie knives,
eye sockets the size of my head. One son
was already starting to plaster. Tissue paper
went on first, to keep the plaster from sticking,

he said, when they finally cleaned the whole thing
in weeks or months of work. Then he laid
on strips of cloth soaked in plaster.
Once the top was done I waited hours
while they dug underneath with hand tools
and small brushes, turned the skull over
on the now hardened cast and did likewise
to the rest till it all was encased, and loaded it
on a small pallet-like skid. My work began,
to get the horses to drag that heavy
new-made mummy down with little jarring
and no breakage through a bad stretch
of badlands to the wagon landing
near where the scows were tethered
to the river shore.
                           There seemed an odd echo.
My grandfather had told how he worked
for several years in the century before
making

Mummy Paper.

He unwrapped mummies
brought over to paper mills on the North Shore
of the St. Lawrence. Tens of thousands, maybe more,
gathered from the Egyptian desert
where they lay like cordwood, and used
as that for fueling early trains, were shipped
across seas and an ocean for the good linen
they were wrapped in, needed for making paper.
Because rags were always in short supply,
many things had been tried: corn husks,
and corn silk; potato skins, and turnips; pond scum

we used to call frog spittle; hay, straw, thistle,
and horseradish; none proved fair,
though poor boxboard was made from peat.
Some thought the mummies were soaked
in bitumen, but he'd popped fir blisters,
worked enough spruce,
and been covered with pitch so often
he thought he knew tree resin when he saw it.
The paper was pretty good quality
but the resin kept it from being white
and no amount of treatment brought it right,
but it was well made linen.
Wood pulp made everything else obsolete,
though that paper eats itself.
Enough resin was in and on the bodies
so they burned with the speed and snapping
of soft wood in the mill fires.
He hated to toss them in. "You could see
their faces; they might have owned Moses.
Every day seemed like Ash Wednesday."
                                    Here I was dragging
very old dead wrapped up fresh to tell their story.

                    One day as I waited
with Sternberg as a crew jackhammered
the overburden off a find, he told me
they'd just dug through two million years
of rock, that from a distance looked like a thick
old book. He said the rock *was* old, but the badlands
had been extant only a few thousand years.
I saw right then that the priest's stories
were just stories. I stood on rocks

older than Eden. I was looking at more years
than the priest knew existed, and giants *sur la terre*
had walked larger and longer than his mind
could travel. He'd told me my sister was needed
in heaven, and I knew that wasn't so,
and his various versions of heaven
had seemed fine torture to a boy.
Sternberg's son told me many of the plants
these animals ate, that filled huge forests by
            an inland sea,
and some of the animals themselves, were buried
and turned to coal, the broad seams rising near us.
I thought of my sister buried in dirt and shale.
Suffering immeasurable weight and heat
beneath the earth to be changed into something
brought back to the surface and burned,
that would be hell if it existed.
He added if coal was pressured
and heated a lot more it became diamond.
So maybe out of hell came the only possible heaven,
a pure thing, that lasts forever, bid up by seekers.
It was as unappealing as any tale,
but had a certain ring. I drove the hips
and tail of a long walker down the way.
Always difficult finding a way, breaks
and gullies, and even open pitches covered
with white sand like pickling salt
and a finer dry silt that rose at our steps
to cover us like corroded battery terminals,
and made our eyes rub dry in their sockets
like ungreased bearings in their races.
The first footprints of dinosaurs found

in North America were thought to be those
of Noah's raven. Some raven.
They found the wing bones of a Pteranodon
that would have spread thirty feet,
wider than the wings of the biplane
we watched once fly over. I carted
great fish, amphibians, turtles,
and what they called psuedofossils,
nodules of sediment that shrunk as they hardened
creating patterns of cracks like turtleshell.
Turtle stones the Indians called them,
thought they had power, like the *iniskim*,
buffalo stones, petrified bone in shapes
they recognized, that had summoned
the greatest beasts they'd known.
"No good now, white man wants them."

In the river valley
I recognized willows and chokecherries;
bobcat tracks in the river mud; beaverwork
and cottonwoods; diving ducks in the current;
harebells, like my mother's neighbor's, in the margins.
A few of us walked out on free days
for sex or drink. The short trail,
but steep for half a mile,
passed a boulder man laid out on the prairie
for hundreds of years.
We walked on needle grass, thin leaves wound
round a thicker, sharp center; prairie wool,
thick carpet of curled grey leaves;
kicked up large hoppers with orange-striped legs;
passed prickly pear nibbled by coyotes,

a place not lost on me, but too easy to get lost in.
You couldn't climb or move in rain,
the whole terrain then was grey clay mud.
Sternberg said the whole landscape, and that man,
was going to wash down the Red Deer River
in time, that the place was eroding
like melting ice cream, millions of tons
a year headed to the Arctic. The river
often looked like mercury. After rare storms,
even when the footing looked bone dry
the next day it gave and weighed. They said such storms
way back often washed away
the weakly connected heads when the neck muscles
of the suddenly buried dinosaurs rotted.
I could imagine boulder-like skulls tumbling
toward distant ice and seas. We rode the river,
horses on flatboats, men in the scows,
drifting from likely site to likely site
in the last great bone rush.

I called Winnepeg

THE CITY OF GEESE

after passing through it two Falls running
coming home. The city would rise
slowly in appearance, abrupt in its stance,
like palings driven against tides of weather.
Both times windy and overcast days
pushed thick fast moving clouds
across flat, grass-flattened land.
Rains had left every slough and pothole
full of water, every one of those was full

of geese, and more were coming.
Far and near, across the entire sky
chevrons of geese sailed in,
sometimes stacked three and four deep
like the wake of some invisible swimmer
in air that was cold, and thick with wet.
As they got closer to the ground,
moving fast, the geese would rise up
wings wide to stall, or twist almost on their backs
to dump speed to land on water
or flump to ground. And what a din
I heard during layover, a traffic-jam-honking
over the widest landscape possible.

I'd hear the same thing some years later at

CAPE TORMENTE

a few miles north of Ste.-Anne-de-Beaupré,
where mother made pilgrimages,
when my father once took me snow goose
hunting there. At Quebec City we'd crossed
the great cantilever bridge, still quite new,
longest of its type in the world
my father told me; dropped my mother off
at the station near the shrine;
were picked up at a further station,
and arrived at the lodge early in the day.
Teams of ponies pulled us hunters
out onto the tide flats on drags
like stone boats with plank seats and gun boxes.
The ponies strained knee and hock deep
in the water-soaked gravelly mud.

Gamekeepers lifted off the tops
of waterproof boxes used as blinds.
We sat with heads at tide level
waiting for the geese to go out and feed
on sand and gravel bars exposed at low tide.
This is where aristocrats belonged, my father
said, but without the boxes.
Swirls of white, and a few blue, geese
rose in great numbers
from the grain fields they gleaned.
Like a snow squall scudding
in front of the cliffs that rose sharply
behind them, they carried themselves
and were wind carried high over us,
then fell on the bars with the same air-braking
and twisting moves I'd seen out west.
We got a few shots at low-flying ones.
Sitting, waiting their return ahead of the tide,
we watched them feed out of range.
En masse they looked like white islands,
like huge ice floes stuck in the river,
the line of shadow around the whole
like the dangerous sunken edge.
The sound the geese made as they fed
carried over the water, a guttural muttering
like wood frogs in their dense spring chatter.
Ducks fed behind us in pools
and entering creeks, and duck hawks fed
on them, ate them right on the strand
because the fall-fattened birds
were almost too heavy to carry.
The water began to rise, so did the geese

in small then larger numbers. We shot
as many as we pleased. Then the teams arrived
to empty the whole row of blinds,
and fill the game boxes to overflowing.
We sold some back to the lodge,
took five with us. My father would hang
them in the cellar, like the fowl he shot at home,
till maggots erupted from their heads
when he'd say they'd aged enough to eat.
I would not enter the shrine on the way back.
My father and I smiled, said nothing
I remember all the way home.

BASEBALL AND NEW HOTELS

drew me to Florida.
The doctor never played after the epidemic,
but he cut diamonds in the field in back of his house;
paid for equipment the boys ordered
from Monkey Wards; drove his big car,
after he traded the buggy, full of players
to other towns, even over the border,
to make games. Great wooden gear boxes
tied to the rear or roof, players arriving tired
from standing miles on the running boards,
players shaking themselves out
after sitting on or under others,
the most familiar they'd ever be.
He drove his son so hard
he'd finally never play
when his father watched,
but the boy had an arm like David's slingshot,
and batters jumped and twisted,
like those touch-me-not pods
we snapped as kids,
as pitch after pitch sped by.
He got a letter from John McGraw
inviting him down to spring training.
We'd heard hotels were being built
on the island fronting Miami;
thought we'd go down and work the winter warm,
then he'd stay on playing ball.
We drove down Route 1 if you could call it that,
what a hodge-podge of surfaces,
most of them dirt. We hit the red clay
of Georgia along with the rain
and couldn't move for a week,

tires just whirled on the rust-red muck.
We stayed in a room behind a gas station
and were glad we weren't black French.

The new mill in town had a steel frame
with the walls hung on, but them hotels
were surfaced with metal and marble
and the kind of shine you see on a movie screen
in the well-lit places.
The hotels rose soft-colored, facing
the sharp ocean light reflecting off them
and the big touring cars parading
down the ocean highway.
Many of those shiny cars were so new
they sat in the parking lot running
for hours to break the motors in.
He worked in the kitchen
and me on the grounds. I kept flamingo shit
off of the lawns and pool edges.
Owner shipped those birds in from the Bahamas
where a pool-boy said they ate them,
he ate them, and I joked about drumsticks
but thought – turkey-sized and ocean fed,
the hotel didn't want to leave me hungry.

When the owner heard I came from Vermont,
had worked on a farm there,
I became head dairyman of the jersey cows
brought south for the winter,
and sent north for the summer
or they'd die of heat and disease.
I milked early and late in a long cool shed

at the back of the grounds;
separated the milk and cream
served at our and neighboring hotels;
put the cows out to feed
in long back pastures
stretching west toward Biscayne Bay.

THE NIGHT CROSSING TO HAVANA

                              occurred because
I often sat with my friend in a room
just off the kitchen where big rollers
played poker and drank rum
run in from the islands.
One player, slick hair, slicker suits,
probably hands slicker yet,
drank milk I brought him for his ulcer,
drank it with rum and sugar,
a strange cambric tea,
and brought girls I ogled.
One night one stepped in thin as a cigar
and as dark, and she was damp
with sweat like a chewed end,
something every man in the room
wanted to lay his lip over.
And this *slick* finally looks around
and hands me money; says "She wants
to go the Havana tonight, take her,"
and goes back to his game.
We take a cab to the Port of Miami,
over the new bridge across the bay,
roll up at Peninsular & Occidental Steamship Co.,
one among others that came and went
so fast at that time, and I buy two tickets
to ferry us on the night crossing.
Port was crowded, even sailing ships
resurrected to carry building materials
south for the boom, like the railroads
they laid across swamp and sand
just to get there in time to go bust
and they bundled them up and trundled them

to the coast to sell to Japan.
Probably some of that steel wound up
in those ships that sunk ours
and wound up sunk in the later war.
We're on the boat and heading out
at a southwest cant, and we cant
up the side of every wave; down the other,
in the trough; and at the top;
and not five minutes out, I'm casting
my insides into the ocean.
She's leaning beside me, teeth white
as the walls of the ship, hips swaying
to keep balance, and for the first while
I can notice that, but soon I'm over
the rail with an ache in my gut
and retching that won't stop
and she starts to quietly sing
a song I suppose a mother might sing,
but in other circumstances might turn
a man into a dithering boy.
She reappeared on deck in the morning
saying we were approaching our landing.
I could barely stand
to look up, but it looked like only land
and a city we were going to steam onto,
no port or opening at hand.
But beside a fancy pile of stones
like the *vieux fort* in Montréal,
and that she called *Morro*,
we sailed up the narrow neck
of the harbor to the larger basin
and I eased myself ashore

down stairway and gangway.
The city lay to the west,
hard to tell if lit by last lights or first lights,
gamblers or bakers
on the wide boulevards rimming the shore.
She gave me a look of pity
and disgust on the quay
then strode toward a jalopy taxi.
Even sick I could see
she began to walk wide,
a new swing to every part
and each lovelier than any part
of the city I could see, though the low houses
along the coast, the lighthouse and castle,
and the white coral limestone of the city
casting back the dawn light,
and the ship-wake white caps breaking
on the green sea wall were dizzying.
The green sea wall holding back the ocean
from the boulevards fronting the harbor
and all the way west like a city dike.
Signs with long names I couldn't make out,
"Prado," and "Malecón," *she* said,
new wide avenues that had taken the old,
that she was going to take me down.
The heat of day rose fast as we rode past
the Legislative Palace, a great fancy pile
that cost her family and every one, she announced,
and swore at some Marchado,
"President of Death."
I couldn't understand the signs
till we came to O'Reilly.

goddamn Irish name in Havana,
and we swerved out of the sun
as we moved from the outer drive
to the old narrow streets of business
and churches – so many churches
many weren't even used as churches anymore.
We arrived at the open door at the end of a plaza
of the Catedral. She could walk right in
off the street, no steps or risers
fronted the doors or uneven towers.
I just sat on a stone under a wrought iron balcony
and watched her back
disappear into the interior
where, she later told me, a Columbus tomb
is marked, but he and the Jesuits
were kicked out for good reason.
That as we passed an old watchtower
crowned with a weather vane
in the shape of a woman called *La Habana*.
"Many come to Havana," she said,
"without seeing The Havana."
Then we were on the seafront of pitted
stone wall and houses, all bleached to a truer white
with the sky like the bluing my mother used
on father's Sunday shirts, sharpening the white
so the tropical sun drove a snow-blindness ache
behind my eyes to the back of my skull.
The Malecón, and we saw women
and men, shed of just about everything,
in the breakers themselves, or fishing,
or sleeping, or eating, and she ate
whatever was offered her and took no notice

of what was being asked. We walked,
but it was her little parade
and she was noticed in passing.
A group of men had built a fire
on the back of a turtle. We watched
with them as, I later learned,
the hawksbill strained to flee
with flippers fastened to the sand,
till the men thought the flames had done
their work and they brushed the fire off
and pried the overlapping scales
from the back of the sea turtle
large as a chaffing dish and,
though they tossed it back
as shell hunters have done for generations
believing the turtles survive to grow more,
just as dead. They'd sell their prize
for tortoise shell jewelry and boxes,
bracelets and barrettes so popular then.
The walls of the club we went to
had the look of sea shell about them,
sea shell and chrome, though mostly I sat
sick in the cloak room – why would you need
it in a city of such heat – and heard
the big brass engine of the band
fire up again and again and ride along
to some crash ending or fade
to a distant land. I could smell
both drink and dance on her.
I knew I was going to have to get
back on the ferry, so my heart sank
like that dying turtle. But the ocean roiled

less, and my mouth only tasted like pennies,
and halfway back she stood in front
of me at the rail, facing out.
She lifted her skirt, spread her cheeks,
and said, "Slow!" quietly,
and her ass seemed as tight and big as the harbor
but I wasn't slow and she gave me
the same look as when we'd disembarked there,
so I walked off the ship in Miami
with the taste of bitter metal
and the smell of hiney and low tide.

That was the last time she entertained me
though I had to take her up the Black River
three days later on a excursion boat
past trees as thick and curled as eels,
and flowers as big as my head,
both over my head and floating,
or petals falling, denting the water
in their windless drift, life real thick
there but all that going on underneath
gave it all a funeral parlor perfume,
and the leaves, big and floating
tight together, looked
like you could graze sheep, but manatees
carried the leaves and stems on their backs
as they slowly rose from feeding
in this wet, dark, pasturage.
"Sea Cows," the captain said
and I could see that, even the grizzled noses.
Then he said the tales of mermaids
came from sighting these,

and I thought, Christ
that'd be the end of some journey,
and the idea of those trips
to unknown shores north and south
threw a kind of sadness into me,
and I knew spending time with Slick's girl
was coming to an end,
that she'd never get out
of the traces with me again,
but all these years later I can still feel
her end in my hands
and see her face –
glancing back towards me –
that'd draw you to some distant places.

A month before leaving,
I rode a dozen miles north
in a

TURTLER'S

truck. Green turtles
were riding high tides onto the sands
and heading into the dunes to lay eggs.
The turtlers wanted mostly the turtles
for the meat in high demand
all the way up the eastern seaboard,
but they also sought a few eggs
for local customers. I remembered
one of the priest's tales of sultans
walking about their gardens
and grounds by the light of candles
waxed to turtles' backs, low light

moving in odd and pleasurable ways,
he said, the cool of night,
a break from the hot eastern days,
when they also broke fast
with meals he'd never read the like of.
The turtlers carried a box
of storm candles in the truck.
I stuck a few to a few of the biggest shells
the size of laundry tubs,
and we went to work hefting the rest
of the several hundred pound animals
onto the truck bed. We loaded several
tiers deep, and felt we'd rolled
in a sweat-sand glue. After that hard work
we had only to look for soft haloes
in the grassy dunes, carry our buckets
to hold under the laying turtles
where they'd dug holes to hold
the hundred or so eggs. When finished,
we let the mothers crawl out
to the hard beach where the truck
could drive, and loaded them too.
I could see this kind of cropping
wouldn't last long.
One fella said the loggerheads
would swim in soon.
The truck rode heavy but steady
on the long sands south
as the blue-green light of dawn
looked like it broke at the back
of the sea and washed right towards us
on waves built out at sea and carried

33

at the end by their own momentum
because the early morning shore lay windless,
waves like they were built
out of church or cathedral glass,
base green, then oranges, reds.
and purples on rising water walls
till they were ground up
and plashed on the sand like whitewash.
To the south the new hotels rose
in their faded-dawn colors
long before we got there.

C.M. never did make it in baseball.
He made it the winter with me
and through spring tryouts
into training camp, his whippy arm
surprising a few, and they taking
his quiet for seriousness, but he wrote
his mother and told her to call
the team and say he had to come home
for family reasons.
                    I guess so.
He'd seen his dream and drove away.
I rode home with him
the fifteen hundred miles
toward the remnants of winter,
him facing his father every mile of the way,
and finally facing him
but not saying why he came home.
When he was killed in the war,
older than most who died,
His mother's gold star wasn't put

in the window, but in the small case
with his trophies and awards,
his bronze star too. He'd thrown
grenades through the narrow slit
of a machine-gunners' concrete nest.
The doctor said with his only child gone
he was out of the queue of history.
He paid for the soldiers' monument
beyond center field, where no one
had ever taken his son as pitcher, so fast
everyone hit him late.

Florida, busted by the hurricane of '28,
not worth returning to even before that;
farms failing; going

INTO THE WOODS

seemed the only option.
I signed with a crew working north
of Logger's Branch clearing
the ridgeline rim of the great bowl
of the Yellow Bogs. The high ground
froze early that year, and I'd gone
ahead with a few others to string
a new telephone line from Wenlock Station
into camp. The cutters, cook,
smith, tenders, cant-dog men,
and other teamsters came at freeze up,
and we had tight snow cover
soon after. A dozen miles in,
we were winter bound. We worked
the steeper pitches as easier pickings

had all been had. Sluice roads
and go-backs were marked
from summer prep, and the tracks
were iced before the snow fell
too deep. By spring we'd packed
the way four feet higher
than the ordinary going.
Never lost a load or team
though only one steep pitch
required a snubbing brake.
One Henky sluiced a load.
Though he could've jumped early,
he tried to bring them down,
but he was haying in a gale from the get go
and no mixture of mercies
was stopping that sled from overrunning
his team, and once they fell
under the runners most of the load fell
on top of him, now Mr. Jackstraw
in a log pile like jackstraws.
The camp clerk had tinctures, bitters,
jalap, and drawing salve
for wounds and ailments,
but nothing to draw Henky back.
The camp Boss called the outside
to let the man's family know,
but *we* buried him.
We drew his horses to a pit
we dug in unfrozen ground
and laid him in on top,
as he'd chosen to go with them.

We were glad for the desert of February,
pure light and cold. We'd rise early
and put our duds on, but not our boots.
Feet'd never stay warm
in tight stiff leather at thirty and more below.
On top of wool socks or felts
for warmth we'd wrap the burlap
of feed bags for grip on the snow
so cold it sounded like teeth grating
when you walked, but no build-up
or melting, poor man's comfort.
The coldest nights we'd hear the cannon fire
reports of trees exploding open as cleanly
as knife split or lightning struck,
whole ridges of good second growth ruined
by the frigid expansion of sap.
Full bellies kept us warm, but pork and beans left
a smog of smell, and sounds like the town
brass band warming up in a crowded hall.

Sundays, us teamsters would mix
a tub of warm bran mash for our team
to clean them out for the week.
I'd slip some molasses from the barrel
the cook used for beans
into my horses' mash for a treat.
And after breakfast in the ram-pasture,
we teamsters often went to stable
and braided their manes.
I'd braid ribbons into my teams manes
and I'd even take the longer hairs
of their bobbed tails and knot them up

with bits of yarn. Then we'd have ourselves
an informal show with the whole crew
turned out in their finest. The festive air,
the lateness of the hour, the horses figured
soon enough no work coming
so then they picked their front hooves
up in fine park trots, especially, the Percherons
and Clydesdales with their leg feathers
flying, their nostrils wide, blowing like steam vents.
The peeled white cedar
log, with the name carved,
stuck over the grave
became the pivot point
in our judging circuit,
so Henky was well trodden
in his journey towards dust,
frozen snow, packed frozen dust. . . .
Cartier had made tea from white cedar
the priest told me, *arbor vitæ*, to keep
some of his men from dying
in their long winter encampment
on the Saint Lawrence north shore,
and it had been the first tree
to make it to the old world –
nothing imposing about it.
Here, big ones lay in the squirt dams,
others drowned in the backup.
Getting planted where you didn't live
was a constant threat in the woods work days,
and I did many a whipple tree jig
to get out of the way of logs moving too fast
or, trigged for a second by a stump
or stone, freeing up and slung in odd directions

as the horses drew them for loading.
Usually fellers laid trees right,
but winds and snow devils could torque
them wrong, or they hung up
in another, and, whatever way you cleared
them, could wind up with you brought low.
I'd stand while the cant-dog men
built my load, sometimes near record
of tens of thousands of board-feet
that others would come to see move,
and I'd sit atop pleased and uneasy,
riding it down through widening clearings
to the landing on pond ice many feet thick.
Thaws in January and the season of Lent
made us teamsters perform maundy
on our horses each of those evenings
to make sure no thrush
or scratches afflicted their hooves.
Horses, men, and a long winter,
we scraped the sides of that blown-full,
wind-stirred bowl, clean.

Moose, deer, beaver, fisher-cats
no longer lived there; porcupines everywhere
girdling trees. We stayed till snow fleas
blackened the snow banks, and blackbirds
jeered in the peat bogs, but left
before freshets ran in every low point,
before the cranes and jacksnipes returned,
before pile-drivers started their *gurr–klunk*
sounds in the work of mating at the bog edges,
just as the timber cruiser returned
to lay out next year's cuts and roads.

What the Timber Cruiser Told Me

"The Nullhegan stayed wild.
The river runs through rough country
and all its branches: Logger, North,
Black, Yellow, and the East, drain big bogs.
I cruised timber up to Labrador
and Nouveau-Quebec, and Nulhegan Basin
reminded me of that. I've eaten spruce grouse
too dumb to move when the tree
they were sitting in was felled;
I've plucked boreal owls off perches
in dropping-stained softwoods,
and seen lemmings like them owls feed
in the north on; picked bake-apples
and crowberries in hemlock-barking season,
all while I cruised for the next years cutting.
I helped plan landings and squirt dams
to carry a season's work down
what are really just streams.
You've slogged down that river's reaches
in summer and it only sogged
you to the waist. The mens I brought south,
if they didn't take one long look and go
to work in the woolen mills further south,
drove millions of board feet of timber
out of those valleys on water stained
dark by the peat of the bogs,
dark as the black coffee and strong tea
the mens drank to stay awake
to every moment and movement.
Some of them didn't make it.
Those logs would be whipping
up and down and back and forth

like every shuttle in one of them mills,
but big as work if one hit you.
They had to be tended out at Stone dam,
and again at that impossible curve lower down
that many have tried to run in canoes,
and failed, till finally they carried out
to the Connecticut rapids called the horse races.
Timber and loggers arrived out together
after a long season in, and both
had a little rampage left in them.
Towns along the river had to watch out.
Took years to cut this region over once.
This river drove us both ways,
into and out of life, and, shining dark-like,
just kept coming."
Once again I spent more time with

THE IRISH IMMIGRANT'S SON,

who'd been my friend since the first day
of school – both small,
both picked on.
"Crush nuts," an older boy would yell
as he slugged one of us between the legs,
or "Targets!" and snowballs,
ice chunks, or sticks of wood
we were stacking for the school's
winter fuel, came flying at us
as we tried to run.
His father had worked for a Vanderbilt,
first in the New York City coach barn,
then traveled with him on horse-buying forays.
Vanderbilt liked the horses along the line,

the cross between Morgans
and Canadian chunks, speed and size
to pull the big family carriages.
They'd stay a month or two
going to village horse fairs
and county fairs, buying and swapping
to end up with a couple dozen to be shipped back
on the railroad on a train
with his personal car,
that had sat on a siding all summer,
coupled to the back.
He'd give his friends two or three spans
and keep the rest till they came north
the following year as trade starters.
As the two men traveled, my friend's father
looked at land and finally settled
on buying a piece tucked
up right next to the line,
a boundary marker obelisk
stood beyond the garden.
The New York mansion cook
came north to marry him.
They worked as hard as they had
in Ireland, but could make a living,
cream, butter, wool, lamb heading south
to big cities on the daily train.
My friend rode the family horse to town
on summer Sundays to play ball,
some boys walked miles,
their fathers wouldn't let them work
a work horse unnecessarily.
I worked summers for the family

and did work the horses hard
though fairly. The father mowed,
knowing every rock or small hummock
that could break a cutter bar guard
or the cutter bar itself,
but I raked, both side delivery and dump,
and liked the precision and boredom
of long circling for one long windrow,
keeping the off horse walking
in the path left by the swath board
as I smelled the span in hand,
the grass cut and crushed,
and the new air of every day.
Sometimes I drove the hay rack
with the new hay loader running behind
picking the windrows cleaner
than a bull rake and pulling them
up the incline to be continually forked
and trod down; no single ricks
had to be cocked in the field by hand
or forked on the wagon and placed
one by one in long chaffy days
in the field. But cocks made
for ease of unloading;
now the whole pile lay on the wagon
as if the machine's teeth had stitched it together,
so harder to toss off into the mow.
They hayed in July. The grass tall and ripe
to fill the barn, not like now –
first crop in June, full of nutrition,
and several rowen crops through
the summer almost as good.

Then it was to keep mostly dry cows
well through the winter. We'd disc-harrowed
the pumpkin patch in late spring
and they chopped up the crop
through the winter to feed the cows,
the milk from those still giving
turned a rich yellow hue.
Each August the family showed cows
and heifers at the fair. My friend and I slept
in the stables, milked in the fair barns
early and late, and got in free.
Except for the cavalcade, when we each led
a cow around the race track
in the grand procession before the grandstand,
we had our days free. We walked the midway
past dart, hoop tossing, and ball throwing games,
and gawked at vegetables and homemade goods
in Floral Hall, and the Grange Hall displays
of villages and farming practices,
all the while noticing the daytime quiet
of the hoochie kooch tents.
We were too young
and poor for

THE GIRLIE SHOWS.

We'd sneak to the back of a tent,
wait till the barker and crowd disappeared
inside, then stick our heads under a flap
behind the stage. We watched the quick
disrobing to poor music
on a windup phonograph,
hips swung sideways and back and forth

with beads at the crotch,
a poor curtain soon raised and tossed;
the flash of fake jewels and real tits,
and then the inside line would form
as each man waited his turn to stick
his face in a snatch glistening
with spit and whatever.
We watched chins working between legs,
and saw the short dangling hair
shining from the lights in front.
The women would bend their knees
for the short ones – often Québecois
down for the show,
who could've hauled furs on tumplines
in the days of the *voyageurs* –
and held hair or ears to pull hard
if anyone should bite. We never saw
all of one show. We'd race behind
the horse barns to jerk off,
while the barkers' overheated talk
sounded down the rackety midway.
I never went once I married,
but they often came to bed with me.

In winter we'd toboggan down
the hill called

THE KLONDIKE,

a steep coast to a facing knoll
that forced you toward the mill stream,
all of it in flying powder
that seemed like to smother you,

and you ended up with a lapful of snow,
or on crust that could scar faces and hands,
and made the run out so fast
you had to bail or hit the rocky brook,
and you might as well have been buried
in an avalanche on the long trek north,
but, Ohhh, when you had a girl's legs
in your lap, arms over them
holding the handle rope,
or your own legs around the girl,
her behind rubbing your groin.

Our fun had been fun but he on the farm
and me back in town were now young

MEN WHO NEEDED MONEY.

He sat by his window winter nights
and listened for engines muffled
by wind and falling crystalline snow
in nail-head-popping cold.
Too cold to be slippery,
lakes and ground hard,
the rummers ran
their biggest runs.
But the hills were tough
on overloaded four- and six-cylinder engines.
Big cars: Cadillacs, Chryslers, Packards,
each sped ahead of two or three smaller makes,
all with short chains dragging;
quick stops to hook up at the bases of hills
and a low-gear grind to sing the whole train
to the top of each rise, then unhooking

to fall toward sea level and the cities.
It was a young man's chance –
fast cars, fast money, maybe fast women –
in a region stuck fast
in the past of the land,
wildlife gone, sheep gone, grain gone,
dairying in trouble.
                    Police watched farms
along the line. A neighbor's son
hid in the cellar once when his car turned over.
Sheriff stopped in asking questions
at supper. The mother went down
to get some cider; surprised the boy
who surprised her. She told him to sit tight
till the sheriff left, then get right home,
and don't bother to come back
for the same reason. She entertained
the sheriff's brief visit, and willed
all her company gone.
Her boy wanted to sit behind
the wide windshield of a big Caddy
pushing through storms, the sharp hood
like a ship's prow taking him somewhere
with the journey's end unknown.
His folks knew enough of his dream
to scrape together tuition
for the state university.

I got involved in the trade only once.
A rusty International truck with soft tires
sat on Main Street two days.
Fella offered me fifty bucks to drive it

to Montpelier. I didn't ask the load.
Wound up honking that son-of-a bitch,
that wouldn't do thirty
with its stake body empty,
down through Hardwick Gulf
and over Buffalo Mountain's shoulder
freighted such that it moved
slower than I could have walked.
But it brought me money I didn't have.
Rode the trolley from the capitol
to Barre where my older uncle worked
in the granite sheds, down from the pink
granite quarries of Quebec, to cutting
the greys and blues of the deep pluton
risen up, worn down toward;
dug deeply into. My uncle dug
into his own pockets to pay a guy
who was going that way
to drive me home. Told him
I had enough, but he said if that were so
I wouldn't be there. I accepted with some new
understanding of depth
but probably not limits.
My father often said,
"My brother's always on top of the world,
and the world always seems on top of me."
I thought it might be rolling my way.

THE NEW MILL

                              rested
on half the old mill's foundation.
Most of the those buildings and works
had run down the river in the '27 flood,
and good big pieces of the dam,
including the penstocks,
parts of the spiral chamber,
molded in the concrete,
that led to the low-head turbine.
The turbine runner's cast iron vanes
had been bent and cracked
as though struck with a giant peen.
The tail race had disappeared.
It took every team of horses
the mill owned, and as many as could be hired
from farmers around, a forty-six horse hitch,
to haul the whole turbine – runner and guide ring –
from the bottom of the volute.
It was something to see –
and a crowd came to see –
those great, caulked shoes dig
in the shale and gravel of the bank
and sometimes knees and hocks
split open on the rocks
as one or another went down
before scrambling up, or got caught
by one of those sharp iron corks
in the general flail, but they pulled it
up and onto dry land.
I held six reins in my hands
and barked commands at four outriders
as I rode the cradle and skids.

We kept the wreck moving till it rested
by the tracks where it sat
till it went for scrap in the war.

We built the dam higher.
It reminded me of the thick grey layer
of clay rock rising up over the river
in the badlands, and we hoped this one
wouldn't erode
in the next great flood.
The old turbine had run one big motor
that spun two hundred pulleys
and miles of belts through several floors
to cutters and presses, saws and knives,
fans and sprayers, lathes and routers,
sanders and jigs. Those tools sped work,
but took appendages small and large,
finger tips clipped to arms sawed off,
and the belts did too, slapping along
at high speed, alligator clinches
pinched and flexed over pulleys
till they snapped and reached out wide.
One end once slapped a man
across the face so he looked
attacked by wildcats.
The new turbine ran with a higher head
and could produce enough power
for motors on every mill machine
with excess to the Village Electric Co.
to increase the grid. The old turbine
had been tapped for Main Street,
stores, and small shops producing

wood and metal goods, and the big houses
lining high street, mill owners, lumbermen,
the local banker, producing snobby offspring
and most of the money circulating in town.
Now we put up poles
and strung wire to Livery Street, Third Street,
Water Street, the first branch of Town Farm Road –
Pest Lane, we called it –
so all in the village had at least a bulb
dangling in the front room
and a socket or two for appliances
they bought on credit.
                              You'd be amazed
the number of hand-rocked washing machines
that piled up in the dump.
Often wooden-tubbed, they went up brightly
in the weekly burnover.
A few years later we built a dam
in the upper village at the head of the gulf
to hold enough water for the yearly lows
of August and February, the reservoir's
reservoir with a small turbine
for the few houses and the cheese factory.
And the REA afforded the town
a chance to power itself.
I helped dig hundreds of holes
for the cedar poles that would last
over thirty years – the new treated ones
will last a hundred – and run the wire
to every house and farm.
People you never saw happy
would laugh the whole time we were there.

One old couple danced in the yard.
For a time after, folks would sit
in their kitchens quietly waiting
for evening and that new shadowy light.
And we, the minor engineers
of that larger miracle, on certain days
when the air lay heavy and still in the valley,
would thrill to the thrum in the lines.

TENDING DAMS

occupied a lot of my time.
I cleaned the gate screens, racks and pinions
of debris washed down in spring:
trees; bridge parts; cans and drums;
or summer thunderstorm floods;
hay bales from flooded fields;
junk from casual embankment dumps
ranging from bottles new and old,
mucilage and bleach, bitters and Coke,
to whole appliances like white rafts;
or everyday flotsam washed or tossed:
newspapers, wrappers, letters,
and, later, new plastics of every stripe.
I cleared the penstocks of similar debris,
including heads and hides from jacked deer,
and several times pulled snapping turtles
from the intake boxes, carefully,
and set them in the reservoir,
or beside the tracks to lay
eggs on the railroad scree.
I set head planks in spring
to add hundreds of acre feet of water,
and controlled the gate settings
for outflow to maintain the river
in its bed, though sometimes in drought
we left it dry so most life
between the dam and penstock outflow
died. One gate busted one spring.
We needed to control that flood
and hold our summer water.
Before I got there, two boys from the mill
jerry-rigged a three-quarter-inch sheet

of plywood and some two-by-fours;
floated it down to the dam;
lifted an edge to get it vertical
and let the water pressure hold it
while they slid it down over the gateway.
They hadn't covered three quarters
of the hole before their would-be gate
broke up like a saltine cracker
and the river swallowed
those jags and splinters
down the dam's throat.
I had them help me pull
the old pinioned gate frame.
We laid in thick hardwood planks
with lag bolts, then used their method
of bringing it like a raft
behind the dam, and by lifting
the top only a little the water forced
the whole thing flat against the back face.
We lined it up with the racks
and wound it down.
Other quick projects like that
gave me a certain reputation
for being able to save a situation.
But I couldn't save the furniture mill.
No one was buying, or could afford
our offerings. Company sold out
and the town felt sold out.
Some fool hauled drums of lacquer
to the dump but didn't tell
so in the weekly burn they exploded
and flared and flew in fiery arcs

and sent the smell over the whole town
just as on varnishing days.
But it looked like the doors of hell's furnaces
had been opened, the grates
emptied on the riverbank,
and after the fires and embers
among the ashes and clinkers died down,
left that entry cobbled with char-robed dirt.

DANCE HALLS

acted as a pressure valve
for much of those times.
One woman stood out
like an ember in ashes.
She drank, and I didn't mind it
at first, husky voiced
and leaning into me hard,
had a face that'd mend mirrors.
She'd come on all storm and stockings
and jumble me all along
like no river ever did
though they might have.
We danced at the Continental
on the watertront of our long lake
stretching up into Canada,
at Grand View over Island Pond,
the Shadow Lake Pavilion,
the Boulders at Willoughby,
and other, small, dance halls stuck
in the woods or along back roads.
The big ones were on the Big Bands circuit,
Dorsey, Webb, Tatum, Shaw,
The Count, the Duke, and the King of Swing,
all that royalty of the day
arrived on the better passenger trains
after hours riding past our forests and farms
for what must have been small potatoes,
but we feasted. We knew they'd started
in New Orleans brothels and Chicago gin mills
and the move to ballrooms and dance halls
made them okay for society, and radio,
where we mostly heard them,

a distant sound of dreams
that even the tall, floor-model receivers
couldn't make big enough
to seem near. On stage
they still had enough of the work and grind
to carry us places we wanted to be.
Why the sound
of one of those bands must have carried
out through the open doors
and over the water and border
the thirty miles to Magog,
past Owl Head Mountain
and Horse Head Isle, even the monks
at Saint-Benoît-du-Lac must have gotten
a certain swing in their singing,
the low moan of horns suggesting
something closer than they wanted.
Sawdust or cornmeal eased the slide
of feet. One man said, "I've danced
on that floor many a time,
but I've been on that floor many more."
And many a face slid
all the way down,
drink and hands everywhere
dizzying the head and air.
I never drank, never wanted
the puking and headaches,
though the forgetting
had its attractions, laying
the immediate past down like overripe fodder
to be burned and spread like potash.
The first time we coupled

she flipped me on my back
on a lake camp cot,
and slid down on me
like a one-fingered glove,
but when she moved
the tightening and relaxing
felt more like a Chinese finger puzzle
and no hurry to figure it out.
She laughed and talked long after.
But in the morning she looked
like black worry, and had her own time
figuring out where she was,
then why she slept there.
I'd marry her soon enough for our trouble.
The camp long since tumbled
and crumbled off its cedar post supports.

BUILDING A ROAD

both we and the town on the other side
of the mountain wanted
took two construction seasons
and more work than anyone would wish
on themselves. By then the mill had gone
downhill, furniture market dry
so fewer loggers needed to supply
the saw, shed, and kiln. The CCC
brought men from outside and inside
to crew work none had done before.
They hired me as foreman
for no better reason
than I'd done the like.
We dynamited back
the hill face and overhanging cliffs.
The blaster we hired could tell
where a separated slab would land,
where a loose boulder would roll
or fly. Said once he could tell a boulder
would snap electric lines
and maybe poles that I sank and ran
a decade before. The blast blew that rock,
the size of a small house, up and out,
and whole slabs sheared;
you could look through that jumble
as if you'd blown up a glass factory.
Like he said, the boulder sank
the wires down like a drawn slingshot,
but nothing rose, three poles broke
and electricity jumped from fatigued copper
to bedrock with a sizzle and snap
and smell of a star bit driving

a hole into granite for breaking.
The blasting shook down the last
of an elderly woman's barn,
the highest farm, in whose dooryard
the original track ended.
Only the cupola stood on the rubble,
topped by a horse weather vane,
Black Hawk Morgan. I asked
to buy it. She had a view
of eastern Vermont someone years later
paid a million dollars for.
"It's the last thing I own
that's pretty to look at."

Each day I brought up what the boys needed
on the back of an old open-cab REO.
Riding up the steep grade
on bald tires, cat piss on the road
and you couldn't move.
Raised the mess tent every night
at the road head, the crew moving
up and across such a steep slope
that if you relieved yourself
at the rear door flap
you pissed down half the mountain.
Good thing we never had any sleepwalkers,
the end of the world was just out the door.
We were working on the crooked
and narrow all right, no place
to turn the truck around,
but fifteen young men could
by lifting and shuffling,
then hope first held it in check

cause those mechanical brakes wouldn't't've.
Most of the work was hand work –
picks, shovels, and iron bars,
men just heaving on rocks –
or horse-drawn stone boats
to move the blasted face
out to an edge for road base.
It rained a lot that summer,
made it easy to move some stones
by sliding them on what little soil
lay up there, but same former loggers
put on calk boots to hold themselves
from slipping down
or going over, and wound up walking
on built-up mud you'd need
a hoof hammer to dislodge.
Finally got the grade good enough
to bring the town's new, powered-grader up
to hone the gravel trucked
to cover the blasted base.
We beat the town from the other side
to the small defile in the ridge
dynamited only a little wider
to let the road pass. Tanker trucks
still sometimes scrub on the outcrops.

The next summer they offered
me a job as foreman of

CANAL CLEANING

and dredging crews down in Maryland.
The furthest south I spent a summer in.
I worked walking through watery air

like days in the steam bending room
of the furniture factory, only Baltimore
looked and felt like a brick lined firebox.
Went north a ways, dredging
the Trenton-to-somewhere canal
and clearing the bushes along the sides.
Decided to fill a lock box with eels
to startle the supervisor. You couldn't
grasp 'em just like that,
you had to have some grass in hand.
Filled the box up to the handle
with the damn things. He jumped
all right, then jumped at the chance
to make some extra dough.
Took the eels into the city
and sold them for such and such a pound.
I wouldn't eat them
and didn't want the money.
Didn't need to be fishing for eels
before, during, or after hours.
I spent many of those hours
in clubs and brothels. I didn't drink
but the men I worked with
drank hard and their exploits grew
larger and larger till they might
as well have been digging across Panama.
Often good music cut through it all,
and sometimes a singer with talent
not just a body to watch move.
It'd rivet you though to see a waitress
pick up tips with her twat,
though some sad too, and you could

interrupt their duties to take
them upstairs. A tablemate once heated
four bits with his lighter and clicked
it on the table corner to get attention;
girl came over and straddled down
to pick the coin from his calloused fingers,
and cried out
when it burned her privates
that weren't private at all.
He offered to take her
to her room and make it right,
but that would have hurt too.
The madam was having none of it,
had the bouncers rough him up
and throw us out. He said she had
a licorice stick for a heart,
which was probably true,
but I saw the black twists of people
and those nights play larger in hard times.

PROFESSIONAL TUG-OF-WAR

seemed a chance back in Baltimore
as canal projects waned. A few teams formed
to perform in small halls and arenas.
They'd set up long, cleated boards,
like loading ramps to cattle trucks,
and we and the other team would take
our places – wiry, fast men closest
to the flag in the middle of the rope,
stronger men strung along to the anchor,
the biggest man, who'd often loop
the line about his middle and heave
himself out over the end of the board
like some sailors we'd see stretched
over their gunwales in the harbor
keeping small craft balanced,
only these guys would've swamped
any craft they'd stepped aboard.
Many of the pullers wore caulked boots
like the river drivers I'd worked among.
Give and take at the start would give way
to two rows of men almost lying down
opposite each other, sometimes the crack
of splintering boards, grunts
and heavy breathing. Your hands would bleed
if you let the rope move instead of your back,
but it made for a kind of glue after a time.
Man by man relief breaks every few hours,
eating and drinking on the line
made for contests lasting days,
if the sudden get go
spectators came to see didn't end it
almost before it began. Settled in,

the pull made your arms ache,
the toboggan-like board, your ass,
and it was poor sport. Only the gamblers
wandered in to check now and again.
One hot afternoon they took a teammate
off the boards right behind me.
Dead of heat stroke. Even I didn't know,
nor the man behind, how long he'd laid there,
or how long I'd laid on his dead legs.
No replacements, so they had us in an hour.
The whole operation never had much gloss,
and it all wore off in less than a year.

Used-Car Salesman

I could hardly get used to the title.
I'd bought the garage at the foot
of the street that featured my parents' shop
at the head. Gas and oil brought in some.
Fixing the beaters most were reduced
to driving those days made more,
but little enough, because people wanted
their machines to run not shine.
I made my first car sale to the fat man
and his fleshy wife who bought
my father's shop. Father'd been ill
a couple years, wanted not to spend
his winters working; custom fell
with cellophane-wrapped bread
on grocery shelves. My second sale
was a Ford Tudor and a little trailer
my parents headed south in.
I had to modify the fat man's Nash.
He wanted a wide wicker door
for ease of entry, and the seat pushed back.
Hadn't driven much. Hung a string
from the steering wheel,
as he said pilots did, to know
when his wheels headed straight.
Backed out of his drive once,
two turns to the left, came back one
and hit a big tree in his yard.
I made money at both ends.

A few of the boys began to sit
around my repair bay of a common
afternoon, talking shit, knocking

back beers, and pissing down my drain.
I didn't like the yapping or the stench.
I wired an old magneto up to the drain pipe
in a night's work, and the first
to take a leak next day
charged up his dick real good,
performed a bit-pecker polka
till the circuit broke.
One late comer too they let get it.
It didn't end the yapping –
Pencil talking about whose oil
he'd like to check with his dipstick,
or whose rear end he'd tailgate.
I was still hot for the wife
so I worked as they bulled.

I tried to be fair in my dealings
with most of my customers,
but I didn't miss my chances.
A well-to-do young soldier drove
north with his teacher sweetheart
a year into the war to meet her family.
He stayed too late to drive cross country
to report to his fort in time.
I offered him a tight price.
Then he stayed till almost too late
to make it by train. He had to take
half the price to get his ticket.
I wore the other shoe sometimes.
Banker stopped by and talked awhile.
I mentioned his fine new car.
He said he couldn't get rations

and didn't want it to just sit.
I bought it. End of day as I left
I noticed the off side was dimpled
as though hit by shotgun blasts
like back in rum-runner days.
Went and told him I'd made the deal,
but what the hell happened.
His pile of hardwood kindling
had fallen against his brand new car.
I could laugh at that, and me
for not getting up out of my chair.
But I didn't look for repairs and options
to nickel-and-dime people,
especially if those were the thin shims
holding them upright as they tried
to move through this bastard world.

The Mill Reopened

almost as soon as the war began.
The new owners put veneer equipment in
to make plywood for every military branch:
for airplanes, gliders; PT boats, and landing craft;
camps, and forts here and abroad.
I went back to running the teams by day,
running my almost defunct garage at night –
gas and rubber rationing rendered me out.
Twenty cutter-teamsters went out every day,
each with a span pulling the small raised dinky cart
that came back as a donkey full,
one big hardwood log. They walked
up into Quebec, never rode
either way and just across the border
would buy one pint of pure alcohol
to nurse each way. Surrounding woods
were clear cut, or sugar bush.
Farmers still wanted their maple orchards,
and imbedded iron spouts made those trees
useless as veneer logs. If the long thin blade
that sheared the spooling logs
hit one, it shattered and flew like glass.
Woodsmen were hard to come by
with the draft, and the draw
of factory work to the south,
so I began to run contract teams,
imported under paper I held
for the duration. Sometimes they'd skip,
and I'd track them into Coös County
or all the way to the Maine northwoods
where they were on their own
and better paid. If they wouldn't come

69

back with me, I'd have the local law
drive them up across the border.
They usually worked their way
back westward then south
to finish out their contract,
but cursing my life and heritage,
and their own.
                Goddamn Riel,
who I'd known since childhood, fell
into

THE BARKING TANK.

The day was dry and clear for Christ's sake.
Pencil sees him tip and grabs his hair
before he disappeared among the logs
they'd lowered in, and hauled him out.
but that was too late. We tried to take
his clothes off, soaked with chemicals,
but skin already began to come with it,
the skin of his hands and chest
now on the ground like parfleche.
Doc came, knelt down, gave him a smile
and said, "Riel, you did a foolish thing.
We'll try to help you some."
His wife brought a sheet
from their house across the street
on the riverfront that we carried
him back to. He'd done the opposite
of embalm himself. Doc shot him up
with morphine and left plenty;
said, "This is the third I've seen.
Ten days. He's going to feel afire."

I sat with him every afternoon
after work. Out his window
the river rolled by beyond the short yard
that every spring held ice flows
the size of cars from breakup,
and some years they drove right through
people's walls, or piled up
against bridges and abutments
such that the Army Corps had to blow
them clear, dynamited-ice spumes and flumes.
   As kids we'd sometimes skated
on the river, not sure where the current-worn
thin spots were. He'd have given
something to sink in that coolness now.
Mrs. Miller brought him blueberries,
climbed halfway up the mountain
to pick them that time of year.
He ate a few and told her they were good.
Blue to black, that was him now.
   After ice storms we'd strap on our skates
and take to the roads, even skating
up hills quite fast, then turning,
squatting, arms around our knees,
trying to hold ourselves steady and straight
heading down those hills at real speed.
You never could save yourself:
banks or bushes our only hope,
but we never broke anything.
He came to the end now full bore,
and it hurt as much as it could.

Rationing

didn't hold such sway
up here. When the wife's relatives
visited, I'd send them back down country
with a gallon or two of syrup,
maybe a few pounds sugared off to crystals,
and trout crated with dry ice –
car trunk full, if not too distant,
or loaded in the baggage car with their luggage –
to extend the rationing coupons.
Mick and I'd always fished
since the days on his father's farm,
but we fished harder those years.
Get our limit of a weekend morning;
give it out neighbors and older folks, fill it again
in the afternoon and evening.
He'd wrangle rides with pilots
in the Air Guard, note new beaver dams
deep in the woods and swamps,
and we'd hike in for a day or two stay.
Fried trout and toast, both swamped
in butter, will suit you three times a day.
We'd dope ourselves against black flies
and mosquitoes and walk long reaches
to South America Pond, Unknown Pond,
Job's Pond and it sometimes felt like affliction.
Though many a evening, during the war
and after, we'd stand out
in an age-old bog just down the road
from the farm. Fellas would often come
by, see us out there, and don vests
and waders to join us. They'd wade
in and start to sink as soon as they hit

the visible bottom. You could drive
a twenty-foot pole all the way down
through that muck and plant mire
and never touch bottom.
They'd thrash back to shore, stare at us,
and maybe attack again
from another point. Same result.
They'd wave and call. We'd never answer.
We made sure no one ever saw us
come ashore into thick cedars
with our heavy creels, remove and clean
our snowshoes and hang them high.
Miles of brook, stream, and river beds
went under our boots, and it looked
a lot like work.

THE SILK TENTS

didn't stand a chance
in those hurricane winds.
Strong for their weight and waterproof
if you didn't touch them,
they lay on us like shrouds by morning
as though we had joined those we buried
in canvas and sheets when we ran out of coffins
for those who had died of flu
long ago.
We struggled out
to a forest flattened for miles.
The late hurricane had headed the woods north,
tops and boles aligned to the pole.
We'd been working along the hard
high terrain of the water divide;
days in, we were beyond warnings.
We could see for miles
and couldn't walk ten feet.
Took three days to cut our way ten miles
with the axes, saws, and brush hooks
to open farm land and roads.
Later in the season, when we went back in,
we found even some boundary obelisks capsized.
Two working seasons to clear a two month stretch,
and yet to have the resetting through long surveys.
We carried tons of cement on our backs
to the remoter reaches, though mules and drays
could maneuver much of the length.
The surveyor had several long shoots
to confirm the markers' setting on the line.
Night sighting to lights the easiest
but if air was rough in dark and light

the evenings evening held calm air
and he would climb a cut-branch ladder
to raise the beautifully machined theodolite
on a green-wood staging high enough above the trees
for twenty or thirty mile sight lines.
The Surveyor and his foreman
had traveled from the St. Croix River
and the whirlpools of Eastport
to the wide cold shore of the Beaufort Sea.
He'd ridden the water with herring seiners
on Fundy's roiling waters
the government once tried to harness
with tidal dams but the backwash
would have reached to Bosten.
The black pool by Lubec had sucked sardiners down,
and nearly him too as the crew neared the barge
to triangulate from marks on shore
that told fishermen which side of the boundary
they could try to extract a living from.
The clapboarded factories now formed
a kind of slow cascade to the daily bores.
Between the extremes he helped survey
through an opera house built on the line,
and an orphanage; ordinary homes
where people cooked and slept
in different countries; an Indian reservation school,
a half mile shot with end doors wide open.
careful negotiation with the chief and head nun,
but usually don't ask but survey
so things move along
and apologize if found out or confronted.
He had one mile shoot in the Rockies

that was mostly three thousand
almost vertical feet. Mules packed
in supplies along those stretches,
and one once went over fully loaded.
The rest of the summer, everything that went
missing was said to have gone over
with the mule. At the end of the season
he figured up the mule had been carrying
a ton and a half of equipment.

The seasons I worked we only confronted work,
like minor loggers we cleared the line of growth,
and, like small contractors, rebuilt whole footings;
repaired damaged tops;
reset markers if river obliterated
or farmer overturned, as some were
to increase the boundary of their farms.
We knocked down poachers' lean-tos,
built near that open animal highway
for moose, bear, deer, and never a shot fired
though one did work for us. We often heard,
as he out-walked us one stride for three,
out-worked us two trees for one,
layered brook trout, caught during break,
in his lunch pail
with wet grass or damp ferns,

THE POACHER'S LAMENT.

"I keep telling the warden I can't poach.
The law says you can only shoot
a moose with .300 caliber or bigger
and I only got a .270 Remington.

Told him I didn't know how I'd do it
with so small a gun. He said I'd managed
to fill three freezers in the shed
in back of my trailer with moosemeat,
and they could prove it was moosemeat,
and a crime to have it. Imagine outlawing
having food for a family. The court fined me
but I wouldn't pay, and warden says they'll seize
my trailer. Bank's already after me,
so for Christmas I gave the old lady a hacksaw
to cut off the hitch so no repossessing
is likely to go on. Yeah, I said to him,
go ahead and move it a cunt's hair,
just like I say to you boys
when you're off on your gauge,
and he says just how much is that,
an I tell him to take one from between his teeth
and measure her up. He says they'll be watching me;
told him that weren't much of a show,
but that he'll have to be on parade in the woods
many a moonless night."

But one night riding with me and the surveyor
hauling the full-track in for repairs
and the surveyor checked a load binder,
the handle snapped back open
and caught him full in the face,
it was the poacher who told him his eye
was all the way out of its socket
and to just put his hand up and hold it
against his face – I'm standing dumbfounded –
and the poacher drove

like a poacher will, and got us to the local hospital
where they put the eye back in with what looked
like a fancy spoon. Poacher said he'd popped
enough eyes out for bait
he figured they could go back in.
Surveyor said he owed him years of career.
Worked with the crew for a number of years.
Laid off every winter, I took up

HORSE TRADING.

I took long swings north of the border
to what the boys called the piss farms,
big farms where pregnant mares stood
in long rows so their urine
could be collected cleanly
to produce female hormones.
The foals were unneeded, unwanted,
and the horse folks practically paid you
to haul them away. I built
a little training barn and corral out back;
always ran half a dozen stock
at various stages. People, some people,
now able to afford a pony for the kids,
especially the little girls. If a girl
came along to look, it was easier
than selling air to a drowning man.
Every day, I'd pick up the young ones'
feet; run my hands over everywhere;
let 'em follow me around the small pasture.
I'd longe the year-olds and up,
and at three put them under saddle,
and harness them up to the carts I built.

Townies got used to seeing and hearing again
horses moving at a good clip on main street.
I built light carts so we moved fast,
anyone as old or older than me
had to pay good attention crossing.
I'd take the woman of the family
out, hand her the lines
to show how tractable
all my charges were, bomb-proof,
except to maybe the trains
that only passed through occasionally now.
Started bringing young work horses along,
teaching them to be handled,
and to handle what was asked.
Lifting those feet was hard work,
but loggers and hippies bought them
for their purposes. Sold a pair
of bright-grey, dappled Percherons
to the common law wife of a blacksmith
over the mountain. Down the other side
on the paved CCC road, my '55 Chevy
wasn't up to holding all the weight back
and jack-knifed at one of the steep curves,
sent everything over and twisting
like a falling cat. She busted her back.
The horses had to be shot
where they lay all mangled.
It laid her up six months.
Took a new pair over for nothing.
She could only look at them
out her window, where she said she watched
bluebirds, and the man she lived with

building a barn right over her garden.
I stood beside her bed, my hat in hand,
and could see the shape of the brace
just below her tits under the sheet.
She thanked me for the horses.
I'd watched her with the earlier pair
before we'd loaded; she had the touch.
"Garden there every year we've been here.
Five years. Is that the biggest 'Fuck You'
you ever heard. Son of a Bitch."
Shocked me, but she was shockingly lovely,
and that stupid bastard finished his barn,
said he was finished with her
and left her for another that looked just like her.
Took the pair I'd brought her,
but he'd originally paid for, into the woods
to draw pulp and for sugaring.
I've felt poleaxed before,
but it made me know my age
that I could do nothing at the beginning
middle, end, or sides of all that.

BREATHING

                          comes harder and harder.
The new Doc says, "Emphysema,
and we may have to cut a cancer
out of your throat." He already took
one leg because of the sugar. I lift
myself up the stairs to my workshop
one step at a time, and thump down
them the same way, like a frog bumping
his ass down banks and across roads
in spring migration.
                          I build carts –
bending long ash pieces with hot water
for thills, then using a spoke shave
to round them right. I use old leaf springs
from cars to give a smooth ride,
and solid bar axles I cut from stock.
I piece fancy seats with dowelled backrests.
I fit the shafts when dry and right,
and paint the whole rig, or varnish
it up and leave it all brightwork.
The varnish makes me breathe hard,
same as going back in the house
with the Mrs. smoking like a ham shack.
If a horse or pony doesn't act up in it,
that cart'll last a hundred years.
It won't take much to outlast me,
but I'm trying. Doc wants to take
the other leg, foot the color of old mutton,
but I tell him and the wife I couldn't
get around, and that's no good.
On the other hand, he wants to cut
my throat, and says breathing
through a tube is a possibility.

I saw a show on Public TV.
about some Pacific tortoise that breathes
through its ass, and I tell him
that's what I'll do if need be.
Nothing's given, but I'm giving nothing
away, and will take all the days,
and pieces of days, I got coming,
though me and those around me
will probably suffer for it.

I feel alone now, and work
long hours that way.
I think of the last time I really worked
out in a crowd – maybe I've scarred
enough of the world to be remembered.

SKI HILLS

         began to draw crowds
around the state. People in town could see
that outsiders could pay their way,
but how to get them so far north,
or south from Montreal. We started to clear
runs on a nearby mountain. The mountain.
I knew the Indian that owned the east
and north sides. He lived at the point
the branch comes steepest off the hill
where it slows in an upland bog
before it piles through the dugway
in numerous waterfalls and rock basin pools
then enters the river in a long black curve.
The old man knew the river.
Really a metis, half his ancestors had named it,
Missisquoi, the other half claimed it,

and they fought each other
and everyone else for its water and land.
I climbed that brook, black pool
by black pool for black-backed brookies
time after time, cleaned them – red as iron mines inside –
and walked out through his narrow dooryard
to the poor road home. Often sat
and showed him my catch without saying a word.
He had little English and worse French.
Taught me how to make a crooked knife
and to draw that knife to make hafts
for every tool that needed one
and I would need: axes, broad axes, adzes,
picks, shovels, spades, hoes, froes, bull rakes,
gravel rakes, dung forks, spading forks,
pitch forks, sickles, and snaths
and cradles for scythes.
We used most of those tools
to strip trails along the fall-line,
though it would have taken
a giant to wield the cradle to catch the crop
that came off the coldest faces
of that mountain, but hardly as cold
as the Indian's in first reaction.
I'd showed him skis and indicated
what we wanted to do,
but yes came two years later
when we moved him to kinder circumstances.
Or the Overseer of the Poor moved him,
to almost the kind of place his father ended in,
and we felled trees and drug out stumps
with a vengeance.

We had a surplus tank from the war
to transport us up and drag trees
and the jerrybuilt plow
down those rough and jumbled openings.
Each day's end, with nothing to slow it,
we took our lives in our hands
as much as those who fought
in that mechanical war room.
Pencil, stuck half way out of the hatch,
laughing and letting the tank roll brakeless,
lags clattering, about to come off the rollers
and drive wheels, and we holding on
for Jesus God till we rattled to a stop
at the log landing. We got the first trails
built for skiers, and set the poles
and cables for a single-chair lift
to haul them to the top to cast themselves down
in what we thought would be a pure flow
of money. But the motors to run the lift
were a drain on the town's grid
so the reservoir had to be drained
to clean the dam and racks and inlet pipes.
The built up muck and debris, all the dam filtered
against its back, would in time
reduce the dam to derelict if not cleaned out.
We mined the mire with horse-drawn scrapers
and recovered, our hands fell to

RIVER SALVAGE FROM SILT AND SLAG:

a poorly built flashboard that had snapped
like a trap through the upper dam floodway pins
and cracked one worker's legs wide open;

human bones, rum runners some said,
others thought – dead from the floodplain cemetery
of the defunct pest farm, where the metis's father
lay dead from TB; hay wagons,
one wooden-spoked, one rubber-tired;
a powered ice saw I'd made
from a Model T, and horse bones
from when *they* fell through cutting ice
for cities to the south; fibrous outwash
from the huge pile of asbestos-mine tailings
that rose above the headwaters
of the western branch;
tin cans of all sizes and contents; drums,
some of them rent when they exploded
in the great fire fueled by old furniture factory
lacquer in the riverside town dump,
an army of rats fled in every direction,
a horde tried to ford the river like lemmings
and were washed and tumbled through the turbines;
kitchen tables and various chairs;
bits of machinery from the cheese factory
that used to turn the river white with whey;
turtle shells the size of punch bowls;
cow bones and calf bones; broken milking stools;
a horse drawn plow, and a set of harrows;
ladles, spoons, dishes of stoneware and china,
maybe from the abandoned farm in the high valley
where the east branch rises in a pasture spring;
beams from covered bridges racked off abutments;
a musket barrel from the time of the first road,
built to invade Canada, but left unfinished;
one arrowhead, one spear point; and annual layers

of leaves, millions from each tree
along tributaries and the main channel.
Most everything would have tumbled
over Big Falls to arrive in this jumble.

As the heap of all rose beside the clean
gorgy bed and was hauled away, the musty leaves
dried and swirled dusty in the heat,
and the stink of history filled the air.

A NOTE ON THE TYPE

The Immigrant's Contract has been set in Matthew Carter's Galliard, a type introduced by the Mergenthaler Linotype Company in 1978 under the direction of Mike Parker. Based on the types created by Robert Granjon in the sixteenth century, Galliard is the first family of types to be designed exclusively for phototypesetting. At the time Carter started to work on his new type, Granjon's work was little recognized among designers; his italics had been co-opted as partners for the Garamond types and his romans heavily reworked under the name Plantin. Rather than attempt a literal copy of a particular type, Carter sought to capture the spirit of a Granjon original, and in so doing created a type with a distinct heft and a dense color on the page, and a sparkle not found in most Garamond revivals.

Composition by Daniel E. Pritchard

Printed in the United States
105032LV00001B/70-72/P

9 781567 923537